The Complete Poetry Collection :

Love, Peace and Harmony

By Susan Gardiner ©

ISBN: 978-0-244-86731-7

Manufactured fascination

Alternative lifestyles

Dysfunctional history native wilderness

Invisible woman

Catholic loyalty

Profound roots

Savvy choices

Poetry in silence

Paranoid states intrusive thoughts

Silent choices surreal ambition

Poetic vision

Coffees in the south of France

Champagne in New York

Warmth in winter

Perspective in darkness

Scripture in gold

Intense emotions

Classy emerald green like angels in a dream

Alternative Universe like The Lost Boys

Sunflowers and daisies gesturing feminine love

Sweet and flowing like Manuka honey

Witt like Dorothy Parker

Acoustic sounds on vintage guitars

Precocious like Albertine Sarrazin

Depth and beauty like God

Words with heart

Cancelled plans stormy nights

A poem for Sophie Lancaster

Soft and quiet like an angel

This mesmorizing beautiful goth

White heat Black garments

Your story touched my heart

So angelic and sweet

So smart kind and meak

Elegance with class

An enchanting black rose

An intriguing girl

Who touched my world

R.I.P Sophie Lancaster

Creative thoughts

Retro shawls curled up

In nature

Nirvana playing

Faith bigger than fear

Things pacify God satisfies

Magic path of intuition

Lily of the valley

Unmerciful servant

Angelic girl

Eclectic views

Conditioned by society

Hauntingly beautiful

Auburn and peach

Talented to teach

Sunflowers and daisies gesturing feminine love

Sweet and flowing like Manuka honey

Witt like Dorothy Parker

Acoustic sounds on vintage guitars

Precocious like Albertine Sarrazin

Depth and beauty like God

Words with heart

Addictive sugar

Hungry for knowledge

Innocent minds

Delayed gratification

Beautiful and bold

Vintage photographs

Significant words

Study intently

Elegant elocution

Obvious illumination

Refusal to conform

Patience to learn

Bohemian princess

Truth meetings

Seeking inspiration

Aspiring to be better

Effortlessly cool

Comfortable with silence

Courage to be creative

Full of references

Important mantras

Committed passions

Haunting prophecies

Symbolic gestures

Sacred souls

Eccentric girls

Push to the break

Beatnik style

Harem pants

Metaphysical teachings

Soulful journey

Forgiveness is key

Pride is for the weak

Motivational words

Joyful moments

Peaceful and quiet

Faith in the Lord

Leading us to our promised land

Judgemental wallflower

Pathological honesty

A solitary soul literature at heart flowing with visions of art

Girl with courage immaculate elocution

Girl with self-educated knowledge

Therapeutic states butterflies with beauty

Words that can heal obsolete confidence

Painfully shy misunderstood

Harmonized gypsy girl immensely powerful love triumphs hate

Words can teach peace

Silent aspirations quietly observing

Wild white horses Alternative woman Truth student promising girl

Judgemental wallflower

Inappropriate thoughts dangerous like lily of the valley

Minimalist needs socially awkward delightfully discreet eccentric and meak

The greatest metaphysician

The immaculate Divine His wonders to perform

The greatest metaphysician Jesus of Nazareth

Over 3,000 promise's He delivers all that is ours by Divine right

Who makes way were there is no way
He reveals Himself in many ways
Have faith study the word
Keep him in your heart

Leading us to our promised land

Carrying us at our most trying times we see only His footprints in the sand

Letting go and letting God

Delight thyself in the Lord

Attractive young soul

Taste like Damien Hirst

Stateside

Vitoria Miro

Classy styles peaceful art

Visits to Whitechapel

Deeply passionate love affair

Thoughts in a preoccupied mind

Slowing down with Mazzy Star

Fading into you

Soothing like sand beneath our feet

Coffees on musty tables books on dusty shelves

Words on faded pages

Thoughts in a preoccupied mind

Candles blowing in the wind Crosses at every door

Marble sides glistening snowballs on the floor

Delicate rays decide the way

Poetic vision

Coffees in the south of France

Champagne in New York

Warmth in winter

Perspective in darkness

Scripture in gold

Intense emotions

Classy emerald green like angels in a dream

Alternative Universe like The Lost Boys

Sunflowers and daisies gesturing feminine love

Sweet and flowing like Manuka honey

Witt like Dorothy Parker

Acoustic sounds on vintage guitars

Precocious like Albertine Sarrazin

Depth and beauty like God

Words with heart

My blessings

Smells of sweet sweat and milk

Virtuous and beautiful

Unconditional love I treasure I breathe and live for these special pleasures

I cherish my precious souls

My angels my world my all

My sacred blonde and brown

Deserving of golden crowns

Hypnotic like the cure

Once bitten twice as shy no longer innocent and pure

On my journey away from the obscure

He understood my silences and pacified my demons

Shared creative artistic desires beckoned me forward

Like the rainbow after the storm

Hypnotic like the cure just you and I partying with books and literature

Mentally stimulating unique spirits

Our Rocky

Safe in the knowledge you would never hurt us

You gave a security that was absent from our lives

A profound charisma that whispered unique one that captured our hearts

An unexpected departure The unspoken grief

Haunting speculation on your new life

Visions danced through my mind

Visions of you being loved valued happy and free

Journaling in nature

Sitting in silence

Quietly observing

Appreciating life

Loving God keeping faith

Happy passions

Beautiful dreams

Talented female

Inked and unique

Appreciation of art

Modern classics

Colourful and sweet

Lips with heather shimmer

Words from sugar and bliss

Smells like red Charlie

Chests of books

Art galleries

Madame Butterfly

My angel up above

A fear of dread

Fed the scissors of the imagination

The unthinkable fate

The invisible solace you sought in all the wrongs place

Hope in the hands of destiny

Rewind the time

I would take half your pain

To help you make it through the rain

Literature Art and Music

My escape my saviour and passion is profound like the beat of my heart

Let go like Krigare killer lyrics cutting words

Mellow blues rock n roll classics

Literature that can heal music you can feel

Are the precious stars that lift me up

He gave me these gifts to share

Unassuming courage to express this powerful desire hidden talents this

There was a portrait of an unjust story

It was I who won and stole all the glory

Albertine Sarrazin

Dulcet fetching like a porcelain doll

A graceful and exquisite soul

Gifted beautiful flower

Classic literature of the 60's

Our pleasant pleasure fill my veins with poetic love

Petite passion my obsession a hidden treasure

In my heart forever

www.ingramcontent.com/pod-product-compliance
Lightning Source LLC
Chambersburg PA
CBHW071917160426
42813CB00098B/549